The Way Back

Volume 1

Editorial: Kathryn Juhl
Cover Design: Aaron Doxey
Cover Illustration: Production art from the film *Pinched*, directed by David Vandervoort, produced by Titmouse, Inc.

ISBN-13: 978-1-7344424-0-3

"I've been thinking about the way, when you walk down a crowded aisle, people pull in their legs to let you by. Or how strangers still say 'bless you' when someone sneezes, a leftover from the bubonic plague. 'Don't die,' we are saying. And sometimes, when you spill lemons from your grocery bag, someone else will help you pick them up. Mostly, we don't want to harm each other.

*We want to be handed our cup of coffee hot and to say thank you to the person handing it. To smile at them and for them to smile back. For the waitress to call us honey when she sets down the bowl of clam chowder and for the driver in the red pick-up truck to let us pass. **We have so little of each other, now. So far from tribe and fire.** Only these brief moments of exchange. What if they are the true dwelling of the holy, these fleeting temples we make together when we say, 'Here, have my seat,' 'Go ahead – you first,' 'I like your hat.'"*

Table of Contents

Safe Space Principles

While your leader will create a safe space for your tribe, there are a few principles every member will need to follow in order to keep the safe space safe.

#1: Show respect to others.
For gatherings to be a safe place and allow us to get beneath the surface and to genuinely connect with those around us, it is important to have an environment of mutual respect.

Respect refers to the way in which we speak to one another and how we support and welcome every individuals' thoughts. If you disagree with someone, that's ok! But the key is to be respectful in sharing your differing opinion or experience of a situation.

#2: Practice confidentiality.
In order to foster a safe space for all, what is said in the gathering, stays in the gathering. If someone offers an insight that you would like to share outside of the tribe, ask before sharing with others.

#3: Don't judge.
Judgment says, "Unless you think how I think, you're wrong." It forces everyone to have the same answers to life. The goal of *The Way Back* is to be heard and seen for who we truly are. This requires practicing tolerance — there is no room for judgment here.

#4: Don't give unsolicited advice.
Have you ever just needed to share how you are feeling and had someone say, "What you need to do is..." instead of acknowledging how you are feeling? This can be a frustrating experience! It can be frustrating for you because you weren't looking for advice - you just wanted to be heard. It can be frustrating for the other person because they feel like they were just trying to help, and you rejected their help.

If a member hasn't explicitly asked for advice, it's best to simply listen, provide encouragement and thank him/her for sharing. If you have advice you would like to offer, first ask, "What would be most helpful for you today? Are you looking for advice or just wanting to share your experience with us?" This allows him/her to be in control of whether advice is received or not.

#5: Use "I" statements, instead of "You" statements.
Directly related to #4, if a member gives permission to receive advice, use "I" statements, instead of "You" statements.

- Example "You" statement: "What you need to do is..."
- Example "I" statement: "In my own experience, what has helped me is...."

Remember, we don't all have the same answers to life. What is right for you may not be right for someone else. So, we can't tell others what they need to do. All we can do is share our experiences and give them the space they need to do what is best for them. That way, we all grow together.

#6: Practice active listening.
Active listening means hearing not only the words someone is saying, but also the complete message they are communicating. To actively listen, you'll need to make sure your phone (and any other electronic device) is put away and that you are entirely focused on the person who is speaking rather than thinking of what you want to say when it's your turn.

#7: Do not interrupt when someone is speaking.
When someone is speaking, give him/her the offering of allowing him/her to fully share their thoughts. Remember, the goal of *The Way Back* is to be heard and seen for who we truly are. If we're interrupted, that can't happen.

#8: You don't have to speak.
While you will benefit more from this experience the more you are able to take risks in sharing and participating, some days you may not feel like speaking. You may just want to be with your tribe and listen to their experiences. That's ok! Speaking up is never mandatory.

How to Use This Book

This book is a collection of sparks designed to help you connect meaningfully and intentionally with the people around you. Each spark includes a curated quote, written passage, and prompt to get your conversation started. Every volume includes a year of weekly sparks.

Kindling pages are also provided throughout to encourage individual reflection and actions to take to connect more deeply and meaningfully with your tribe and the world around you.

Step 1: Collect your Sparks
We recommend each tribe member have their own book. Many members (especially introverts) will connect more deeply by reading along in gatherings and having the sparks and kindling for reference outside the gatherings.

Step 2: Choose a Time
Your tribe can meet whenever it works for everyone. We recommend meeting once per week (same day and time each week if possible), allotting 30 minutes from start to finish.

Step 3: Lead with Confidence
The *Getting Started Guide* provides tips for creating a safe space and facilitating in such a way that each person feels seen and heard. You can access this at http://thewaybackmovement.com/.

The Way Back is a shared practice that cultivates meaningful connection and allows us to be heard and seen for who we truly are. By starting this tribe, you're giving the gift of connection and belonging to those around you, as well as yourself.

Throughout your journey, you'll likely get ideas for sparks that would resonate with others. When that happens, feel free to substitute your idea as a spark at your own gathering. And to make even more of an impact, submit your idea at http://thewaybackmovement.com/ for consideration in a future book volume. If your idea is selected, we will reach out and work with you to write a brief description of yourself to include with your idea's publication (or publish anonymously if you prefer).

Thank you for being part of *The Way Back* Movement!

Week 1

Allegory of the Cave

"The world as we have created it is a
process of our thinking. It cannot be
changed without changing our thinking."

— Albert Einstein

The *Allegory of the Cave*
was a dialogue written by
Greek philosopher Plato. It
begins with a group of
prisoners in a dark cave,
dimly lit by a fire. These
prisoners are chained to a
wall and have never seen
the world outside of the
cave. They can see shadows
on the wall by the light of

the fire, but they've never seen the actual objects making the shadows. All
they know are the shadows themselves. So, if they see a shadow of a book,
they might say, "Oh, there's a book." But really, it was the shadow of a
book, not the book itself. It's a bit like knowing the word "strawberry"
means a small red fruit, but never having actually tasted a strawberry.

This allegory reminds me of how we often don't know what we don't know.
For so long, I had never traveled outside of my home state of Tennessee. So
my perspective was very limited. Then, when I traveled to Denver, I was
shocked to see folks eating fruit and hummus at outdoor events rather than
fried chicken and potato salad, which was much more common where I
grew up. And I had heard of the Rocky Mountains, but we had the Smoky
Mountains in Tennessee. At the time, I thought, "Aren't all mountains the
same?" And it turns out that they aren't.

What else don't I know? Well, I ... don't know. With each experience, our
perspective gets a little broader, the color fills in a little more. How can we
free ourselves from only knowing something by the "shadows" instead of
the actual thing itself? Experience. Step your toe in the water. Do something
new.

This goes for people, too. If you have an "other," maybe it's time to learn a little more about them instead of knowing them through the "shadows." Unlike the prisoners in Plato's allegory, we have the key to free ourselves and to experience life in color. Take a step today to experience it in real life, full of color.

Today's Prompt: What is something you may only be experiencing through a "shadow"?

Week 2

Are You Misusing Your Mind?

"Don't believe every worried thought you have.
Worried thoughts are notoriously inaccurate."

— Renee Jain

 A friend was recently talking through a major life decision that was potentially coming up for her. She was feeling overwhelmed, terrified, anxious, and stressed. As I listened, I noticed something: She was piling on all of the potential problems that she may ever face into that single moment.

Why was this happening? The mind loves to problem solve. And it's good at it! So, it comes up with many things to chew on (worry), all of which take you out of this moment.

It might sound like:
- What if I don't have all the answers in that meeting?
- Will traffic be bad on the way to my appointment and make me late?
- My car sounds different today—what if it breaks down?
- What if I never find "the one"?
- What if he/she won't marry me?
- What if he/she divorces me?
- What if my children struggle when they are adults?
- What if I don't make enough money to pay my bills?

It's not that these things aren't important. But the mind is a tool that needs to be used properly and at the right time. If you get worked up into a frenzied state of anxiousness, it's very difficult to think clearly from this state. The question I often ask myself is, "Is this a problem that my mind can solve *in this moment*?" If the answer is no, then I know that I'm living in the future and need to shift to this moment by becoming still and breathing.

Today's Prompt: What do you do when you're feeling anxious or stressed?

Week 3

Look for the Helpers

"When I was a boy and I would see scary things
in the news, my mother would say to me, 'Look for the
helpers. You will always find people who are helping.'"

— Fred Rogers

It can be overwhelming to watch the news or listen to the radio and hear about all of the things going on in the world. There are so many difficult situations and a lot of divisiveness. But for this moment, let's focus on the good that occurs even in the most difficult of situations.

Helpers come in all varieties. They are people who care. People who make an instant decision to get involved and help others. Helpers look like:

- Jonathan Smith, a father of three, who risked his life and carried 20 of his fellow concertgoers to safety during the Las Vegas shooting
- The firefighters who risked their lives to save others during 9/11
- Ian Grillot, who risked his life to save two Indian men when a gunman opened fire on them in a bar
- The everyday heroes who save their neighbors from floodwaters during hurricanes
- Chef José Andrés, who built a team and cooked day and night to help feed the people of Puerto Rico after Hurricane Maria

Who has been a helper in your life? Maybe it is someone who encouraged you during a really difficult time. Maybe it is someone who brought you food when you lost a loved one. Maybe it is someone who helped you see the potential in yourself. Or perhaps it is someone who didn't judge you and just loved you for who you are.

Today's Prompt: When have you noticed a helper in the midst of a catastrophe? Or who has helped you in your own time of crisis?

Week 4

Gratitude Equals Abundance

"When you are grateful,
fear disappears and abundance appears."

— Tony Robbins

Have you ever had those days when you felt you didn't have much going for you? Maybe you were having a particularly rough week at work, which spilled into things at home, and you just felt over it. We've all had those periods of time. But in those moments we have a decision to make. We can focus on the things that are going wrong, and if you believe in the law of attraction, get more of those things. Or we can stop to reflect on all of the things we're grateful for, which creates a feeling of abundance.

A few years ago, I wrote down my "three grateful things" each day, and they would often include things like family, friends, and health—super generic stuff. And then I would be walking around outside and see someone who was blind and walking through downtown, navigating other pedestrians and tons of traffic. In that moment, I would feel a deep gratitude for the ability to see. But for some reason, it took being reminded to be grateful for my eyesight—something that helps me get through every single day!

What small victories or everyday occurrences might you have forgotten or be overlooking when reflecting on what you're grateful for? Remembering these is how you create the abundance mentality! These things might include:

- Your mental ability to be able to work
- Music
- A book you're reading
- The person shoveling snow on the sidewalk in the winter
- Clean drinking water
- Peripheral vision

- A cozy blanket
- Spending time with a loved one
- Someone's sense of humor
- A great night's sleep
- An incredible meal
- Fridays!

Have you ever wanted something, like a job promotion or a partner, and then gotten it? After a while you might have a tendency to forget how much you wanted it in the first place and then gratitude goes right out the window! Today is a reminder to take a few moments to be still and be grateful.

Today's Prompt: What are you grateful for? What tips do you have for practicing gratitude?

Week 5

The Pot Roast Story

"Millions saw the apple fall, but Newton asked why."

— Bernard Baruch

A mother was preparing a pot roast for her family's Easter meal while her young daughter helped. Knowing that her daughter was very curious, the mother explained each step. As she was preparing to put the pot roast in the oven, the mother explained, "Now we cut the ends off of each side of the meat." As young children often do, the daughter asked, "Why?" The mother thought for a moment and replied, "Because that's the way it's done. That's how your grandma did it and that's how I do it."

Not satisfied with this answer, the young girl asked if she could call her grandma. The young girl called and asked, "Grandma, why do you cut the ends off the pot roast?" Her grandma thought for a moment and said, "Because that's the way it's done. That's how my mom did it and that's how I do it."

Still not satisfied, the young girl called her great grandma, who was now living in a nursing home. "Great grandma," she said, "Why do you cut the ends off the pot roast?" Her great grandma said, "When I was a young mother, we had a very small oven. The pot roast wouldn't fit in the oven if I didn't cut the ends off."

When reflecting on your current processes, do you take things for face value or think, "Why do we do it this way? Is there a faster, more efficient way of doing this task?" I once worked with a department that had to manually run reports every day. This process was lengthy and often caused the staff to work very late and sometimes on weekends. Someone once commented to the department, "Can't you just automate those reports with a script?" They admitted the thought of automating the reports had never even crossed their mind. While automating reports would require them to learn a new skill, the hours it would save would free them up to do other things and get them out of the office earlier!

Today's Prompt: Are there things in your life that "have always been done this way" that could potentially be done more efficiently or better?

Week 6

When You Try, and You Try, and You Try

"Yeah, you don't know what it is like when you try,
and you try, and you try, and you don't ever get there!
Because you were born perfect and I was born like this."

— Sam (character from *I Am Sam*)

In the movie *I Am Sam*, a mentally handicapped father, Sam, fights for custody of his seven-year-old daughter. Despite having a huge support system and being an incredible father, a social worker visits their house after his daughter, Lucy, tells a friend at school that she's adopted. The social worker determines that the environment is unfit for Lucy and removes her from the home. At this point, Sam has a huge uphill battle to get his daughter back.

During this incredibly emotional and difficult time in Sam's life, he faces many challenges. He wants a good lawyer, but he doesn't have enough money to pay for one. Most of his friends are also mentally handicapped and aren't able to be convincing character witnesses in court. The only other person who could testify, Lucy's godmother, hasn't left her home in years and doesn't feel she is capable of leaving her house, let alone testifying in court. A lawyer decides to take on his case pro bono, but the trial is so difficult that Sam breaks down, convinced that he is not capable of taking care of his daughter. While Sam temporarily gives up, he ultimately presses on to stay in his daughter's life.

Have you ever felt like you're trying *so* hard, but just can't seem to get "there"? Sometimes, it might feel like giving up is the only answer. So what are some things we can do when we feel like we're trying as hard as we can, but getting nowhere?

- **Remind yourself that you're a human *being*, not a human *doing*.** Sometimes, you'll be super productive. Other times, you won't. It's an ebb and flow. If you need to sit and do nothing for a period of time, do that.
- **Leave it alone for a while.** Creating some mental space between you and the "thing" can sometimes bring fresh inspiration when you begin working on it again.
- **Feel the "feels."** Think about how you will feel once you've accomplished the thing. Remember what prompted you to start the endeavor. This can help increase your energy and give you a push forward.
- **Don't compare yourself to others.** Nothing will zap your energy like comparing where you are to where others are. While you are intimately aware of your own setbacks and failures, you have no idea what others have gone through to get where they are.
- **Touch a tree.** Feel the sunlight, touch a tree, smell a flower— whatever. Sometimes, we forget to breathe and simply be.

Lastly, remember you aren't alone. We all go through times of discouragement. Surround yourself with positive people and things.

Today's Prompt: When was a time you felt like you were trying so hard, but just couldn't seem to get "there"? What did you do to overcome the feeling?

KINDLING

Share the spark.
Light new kindling.
Keep the flame aglow.

Don't wait until people are dead to give them flowers.

— Sean Covey

Flip this page over to take a step to connect
with the world around you.

Gratitude Cards

I've had many incredible managers in my career. I have struggled with confidence for quite a long time, and each of them told me what they saw in me. One in particular made me rethink the impact I make on those around me. He asked me if I was interested in becoming a leader in the organization, and I told him that I wasn't sure I could be that. He told me in very clear terms that I already was a leader and how my positive attitude affected those around me. He highlighted my strengths and how they could be used to benefit the company, others, and ultimately, myself. In this conversation, he helped me see my future self.

What if he hadn't shared his thoughts with me? Would I still be a leader? Probably. But his words stick in my mind when I'm feeling inadequate or feel like giving up. They help provide me with the drive to keep going because I know his words are true.

The great thing is, it wasn't just *me* that got something out of the conversation. He did, too. Psychologists have scientifically proven that one of the contributing factors of how happy you are is how much gratitude you show. In fact, if you write down why you're grateful for someone, your happiness will increase 2–4 percent. If you tell them, your happiness increases 4–19 percent.

Action: Get some gratitude cards (index cards—use your imagination) and write a quick note to someone(s). The note should include one of the following:
- **Why you're grateful for them**
- **What you value in them**
- **What you admire about them**

Week 7

The Messy Middle

"The middle is messy,
but it's also where the magic happens."

— Brené Brown

A friend of mine is in the middle of a very messy divorce. Her husband was very abusive, and once things got to the point of being too dangerous for her and her children, she left for good. This is the period of time she has always feared. It's why she never stayed gone for very long when she left in the past. While she's in the middle of

custody and financial arguments, she's also in the middle of trying to figure out who she is, what she wants to do in life, and how to best support her children and herself.

While there has been a ton of lows during this time, there has also been many highs. As she took her little boy to his first day at his new school, he looked around at the other moms and then looked at her. "You don't look like all the other moms," he said. Instantly, she thought she knew what he meant—that she was disheveled, not as put together as the other moms. That they knew where they were going, what they were doing, and stepped forward with confidence that she just didn't have in this moment. "What do you mean?" she asked. "You're so much more beautiful than all the other moms," he replied.

It's probably safe to say that you're in the middle of something in this moment as well. Maybe you're in the middle of a project, or in the middle of learning something like how to play the piano, or in the middle of a health journey. Some days, the middle will feel amazing! You might nail a presentation for the project you're working on, or hit the really difficult note you've been practicing all week to hit, or you might see the dip in the scale that you've worked so very hard on. And other days, things might not be so good. You might hit a roadblock on the project, come across a chord that you just can't get right, or see an increase in the scale when you step on it.

The middle is messy. For all of us. There will be ups and downs, guaranteed. But without it, no progress would occur. Every good day, every bad day, the entire messy middle leads you through the journey that you will one day look back on.

Today's Prompt: What is something you're in the middle of at the moment? Have you found the middle to be messy? What do you do when you have a rough day in the middle of an endeavor?

Week 8

Everyone Believes They Are the Good Guy

"Everyone believes *they* are the good guy."

— Amaryllis Fox (former undercover CIA Officer)

A few days ago, someone wrote a snarky negative comment on my social media page. Because most people who are involved in this movement are positive, thoughtful, insightful folks, almost all comments are positive and uplifting. So this comment caught me off guard. My immediate thought was, "What a horrible person! What kind of awful life have they had that has made them act this way?" My mind started imagining what they looked like— maybe a hunchback with fangs or a long pointed nose. Assumptions about them, such as "maybe they hate kittens, too," crept into my mind.

Then, I looked at their profile. And I was shocked. They were a normal looking, seemingly fun-loving person. They had children who they seemed to really love. They had a picture of them hugging their dog while smiling. Their posts were inspirational and uplifting.

Confused, I sat for a while, just thinking. It was during this time that I came across Amaryllis Fox's video about her time as an undercover CIA Officer. In the video, Fox discusses why so many of us misunderstand each other. We simply don't take the time to listen or understand another perspective. She states, "The only real way to disarm your enemy is to listen to them. If you hear them out, if you're brave enough to really listen to their story, you can see that more often than not you might've made some of the same choices if you'd lived their life instead of yours."

Instead of simply judging someone, taking time to understand his or her perspective is key. Maybe the person who posted on my page was having a horribly difficult time at work, or maybe they were having relationship problems. I've had many off days when, if I judged myself by a single incident or moment in time, I may have thought I was the "bad guy." Thankfully, I have context and insight into my perspective, so I avoid judging myself based on a single moment or act. But so often we don't give others the same grace.

Today's Prompt: Have you ever judged someone without taking time to understand his or her perspective? Have you ever felt judged by someone based on a single incident or moment?

Week 9

What Is Your Why?

"When we know *why* we do what we do,
everything falls into place."

— Simon Sinek

Sir Christopher Wren, who designed St. Paul's Cathedral in the 17th century, was one of the greatest English architects in history. As the cathedral was being built, he would walk through it to check on the progress. One day while walking through the cathedral, he stopped to chat with a man who was working on the cathedral. He asked the man what he was doing. "I am cutting a piece of stone," the man replied. As Wren continued walking, he asked another man, "What are you doing?" The second man replied, "I am earning five shillings two pence a day." Wren continued walking and came upon a third man. He posed the same question. The man replied, "I am helping Sir Christopher Wren build a beautiful cathedral."

Some days, it may feel like what you do doesn't matter. It might be easy to get in a rut and think, "All I do is run reports" or "I just stay at home with the kids." But what you do directly impacts the bigger picture. It's crucial to understand the greater vision and how you impact it.

In *Start with Why*, Simon Sinek explains how understanding your own why is so powerful. He states that, "Until I discovered, articulated, and began to focus on bringing my Why to life, I was out of balance."

Sinek provides a simple activity to define your own why. It's two small fill-in-the blank lines, but oh so powerful. I'll share my own example below:

your contribution
↓
To encourage and inspire others through The Way Back
So that people will feel valued, heard, and connected.
↑
your impact

Today's Prompt: What is your "why"?

Week 10

Listen More Than You Talk

"Most of the successful people I've known are the ones who do more listening than talking."

— Bernard M. Baruch

During a conference I attended, we were split into pairs of two and given a task without knowing the end goal. The instructions were for one person to tell about a time when he or she felt confident and what made him or her feel that way. When the time was up, as it was explained to us, the other person would tell about a time when he or she felt confident.

My partner told about a time when she was an Administrative Assistant for a high-tech company. Every morning, she was expected to send out updates and the lunch menu for that day. She found out that most people were deleting her emails without reading them, and she wanted to do something about it. She was a very talented artist and loved to draw. So, each day, she decided to draw a funny cartoon or inspirational quote and attach it to the daily update and menu. People loved it! It was a fun way to start the day and she began feeling much more confident.

When the facilitator announced that the time was up, we all expected that the other partner (in this case, me) would share a story about a time when we felt confident. But to our surprise, the facilitator asked us to now use this time to repeat back to the original partner the story that they had just explained, using as much detail as possible. The true exercise was being a good listener. If a partner wasn't paying attention, and instead used the time to craft their own story about when they felt confident, they weren't truly listening. It was an interesting exercise and demonstrated what so often happens in conversations.

Today's Prompt: Are you a good listener? If you were quizzed on what someone just told you, would you be able to repeat it back or do you spend that time crafting what you will say next?

21

Week 11

The Keeper of the Spring

"I am only one, but still I am one. I cannot do everything, but still I can do something; and because I cannot do everything, I will not refuse to do something I can do."

— Edward Everett Hale (*The Man Without a Country*)

What difference do you make? The late Peter Marshall, former chaplain of the US Senate, told a parable in the late 1930s that may help you answer this question.

The parable, titled "The Keeper of the Spring," centered around an elderly gentleman who lived high above an Austrian village in the Alps. A few years earlier, the man had been hired by a town councilman to keep the stream from the mountains to the town clear so the townspeople would always have fresh water.

The town always had cool, refreshing water due to this man clearing out debris and keeping careful watch over the entire stream. If a big storm came, he would work tirelessly and remove any branches or obstacles it put in the stream's path.

As the elderly gentleman was working high above the village, the townspeople had almost forgotten he even existed. The village itself was beautiful, with the crystal clear water, naturally irrigated farmlands, and charming restaurants.

One evening, as the town council was reviewing their budget, a council member asked about a line item for a salary of a "Keeper of the Spring." The councilman said, "I don't understand what he actually does. Has anyone even seen him? I think our money could be better spent elsewhere. Do you agree?" The council unanimously decided to remove the "Keeper of the Spring."

At first, nothing really changed. The townspeople went on as they always had, with fresh, clean water. But in the fall, the leaves began to change and then fall off the branches, as they had done every year. The leaves began to accumulate in the stream and started causing a mucky, sludgy, slimy, smelly mess.

In the village, people couldn't believe that their beautiful water source had turned into such a horrible mess. Water was scarce and many people fell ill. Tourists stopped coming and the economy went downhill. The town council called an emergency meeting to determine what was going on. After a few minutes, they realized that the one major thing they had changed was removing the "Keeper of the Spring." They immediately rehired the elderly gentleman and within a few weeks, the stream was clear again. Everything was back to normal—the townspeople had clean drinking water, tourists started coming back to the village, and the economy was doing well again.

Sometimes, when I think about the great needs of this world in comparison to my abilities, I feel overwhelmed. But this parable is a great example that no matter how seemingly small your action, a great deal of good can come from a single individual. Whether it's listening to someone and making him or her feel heard/understood, or packing a lunch for your kids, or creating spreadsheets that keep everyone organized, or clearing debris out of a spring for a village, *you* make a difference.

Today's Prompt: Have you ever felt discouraged when thinking about the great needs of this world in comparison to your abilities? Does this parable help? What one thing can you offer to others?

Week 12

The Voice That Doesn't Use Words

"There is a voice that doesn't use words. Listen."

— Rumi

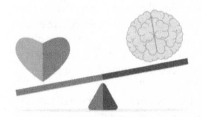

Have you ever thought about someone and felt like you should call them, but didn't know why? Or maybe you were house shopping and when you walked in a particular space, you thought, "This just feels right." Whether you call it intuition, your higher self, the universe, etc., it exists. It can sometimes be difficult for our minds to rationalize or understand it, but it is definitely there.

I recently made a business decision that was wrong for me. The interesting thing? I knew it was wrong the moment I made it. But it was the logical thing to do. On paper, it made sense. And my gut reaction, or intuition, did not make sense. After I made the decision, I kept telling myself it was the right thing to do and everything would work out. Weeks went by and things weren't working out the way I wanted them to. But I kept telling myself to "stick in there" and just move forward. People would ask how the situation was going and, with a smile, I would say, "Oh, it's going ok! Sometimes these things take a little longer than we want them to." Then I would silently cringe because I didn't believe my own words. But I wouldn't back out because I would be forfeiting quite a bit of money.

I wanted things to work out so badly that I tried forcing them. But every time this decision brushed up against me, the reality that it was wrong for me was apparent. I had expended tons of mental energy on this one single decision. One day, I woke up and stared at a quote on my wall. The quote said, "Anything that costs you your peace is too expensive." That was it. I reversed the decision that day, forfeited the money, and felt such a sense of relief and peace.

Today's Prompt: When is a time you made a decision based on intuition? How did it work out? Do you often take your intuition into consideration when making decisions?

Week 13

Failures of Kindness

"What I regret most in my life are failures of kindness. Those moments when another human being was there, in front of me, suffering, and I responded ... sensibly. Reservedly. Mildly."

— George Saunders

One of my all-time-favorite speeches is the convocation speech by George Saunders at Syracuse University for the class of 2013. In this speech, Saunders shared his greatest regret. He mentioned many things that he could regret, such as times when he felt humiliated, odd jobs he had worked, and a very  interesting skinny-dip in a river during which he looked up and saw about 300 monkeys pooping above him (into the river). But none of these were his greatest regret. Instead, his greatest regret was failure of kindness.

He went on to share a story of a young girl who he saw being bullied by classmates when he was in school. While he was nicer to the girl in comparison to others, he reflected on how she must have felt and how difficult this time must have been for her.

He imagined conversations between her and her mother, where her mother asked how her day was and if she was making lots of friends. He assumed that she probably told her mom everything was great and she had tons of friends and how she had to hold all of the hurt inside.

Ultimately, he wondered what happened to this girl. He wished he had acted more compassionately toward her when he had the opportunity. In this speech, he encouraged the graduating class to look at the people in front of them and to simply be more kind.

Today's Prompt: Is there an area of your life where you may need to apply Saunders' advice to look at the people in front of you and simply be more kind?

Week 14

Keep Your Face Toward the Sunshine

"Keep your face always toward the sunshine—and shadows will fall behind you."

— Walt Whitman

One day in late fall, I was walking my dog around the block. There are a few trees downtown where I live, which we both love. I love looking at them and he loves ..."watering" them. It was a beautiful, crisp day out, with tons of leaves all over the ground. Most of the trees had no leaves left.

However, one tree was different. It seemed to be split down the middle. A couple of dead, brown leaves were on one side. Most of the other leaves were gone. But the other side had several beautiful, green leaves. I thought, "How are these leaves still alive?" After staring at it for a couple moments, I realized that those leaves were facing the sun. This made me reflect on how being intentional about what we surround ourselves with and positivity is incredibly important for our health and growth.

Just like these leaves, it is important for us to "keep our face toward the sunshine." For me, that means covering my apartment with inspirational quotes, hanging out with people I admire, cultivating a work experience that is peaceful and joyful, watching uplifting movies, and reading books to learn and grow. What about you?

Today's Prompt: What are some ways you "keep your face toward the sunshine"?

KINDLING

Always laugh when you can.
It is cheap medicine.

— Lord Byron

Flip this page over to take a step to connect
with the world around you.

Laughter Is the Best Medicine

Laughter has some incredible health benefits ("Stress management," 2016). Laughter:

- Relieves stress
- Improves the immune system
- Relieves pain
- Soothes tension
- Improves mood

When was the last time you laughed? I don't mean a chuckle. I mean the kind of laughing where your eyes are filled with tears and you're gasping for breath. If you can't remember the last time you did this, it's time to make it happen!

Action: Schedule a happy hour, karaoke night, or some awesome outing with your tribe. Discuss when and where you'll go.

Week 15

Perfection

"Imperfect action is better than no action at all."

— Jared Lichtin

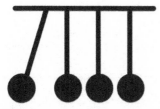 Recently, I participated in an improv session with some members of my online community. The facilitator walked us through several exercises that were meant to spark creativity and help us shift into a brainstorming mentality.

The instructions for one exercise was to make a silly face and then call out someone's name. That person would then copy the silly face, then make a new silly face and call out another person's name. It was going smoothly until my name was called. I copied the person's face that called my name and then it was my turn to make a new silly face for someone else to copy. And I froze! I couldn't come up with a great silly face. I just sat there, on video, not moving at all. I've not had much practice at making silly faces in a while and I didn't know what to do. Finally, the facilitator paused the session and said, "Patti is trying to be perfect. But there's no such thing for this activity! Any face you come up with is exactly what we need!"

Sometimes, you just need to take action. Whether you are starting a new project, beginning an exercise routine, or learning a new skill, imperfect action is better than no action at all. You may not know exactly what to do, but any action or step you can take will often provide the momentum you need to get started and keep going.

The worst thing you can do is stay stuck. One of my favorite quotes by Eckhart Tolle is, "Any action is often better than no action, especially if you have been stuck in an unhappy situation for a long time. If it is a mistake, at least you learn something, in which case it's no longer a mistake. If you remain stuck, you learn nothing."

Today's Prompt: Is there something you are waiting to take action on when you know exactly what to do rather than taking imperfect action? What might happen if you take one small imperfect step rather than waiting on perfection?

 Reader-Submitted Spark Idea
Today's spark idea was submitted by Jessica Jacobson of Denver, CO. Jessica is a Transformational Coach, Mentor, and lover of all things that empower women.

Have an idea for a great spark? Submit your idea at TheWayBackMovement.com.

Week 16

When You Don't Know What's Next

*"When you've exhausted all
possibilities, remember this: You haven't."*

— Thomas Edison

Sometimes, it's easy to know what the first step of an endeavor is. If you want to write a book, start writing. If you want to improve your health, go to the gym. If you want a promotion, apply for it. But what happens when you get writer's block while writing the book? Or when you aren't seeing the improvements you were hoping for even though you're working out regularly? Or when you find out you aren't getting the promotion? What do you do next?

Maybe take a nap? That's often been my solution, although it's never actually done much for me besides making me more rested. But here are a few ideas I can offer that may actually be helpful when you don't know what's next:

- **Surround yourself with people who lift you up, like a *Way Back* tribe.** We come from tribes—it's how we're meant to live! But so often we suffer in isolation and stay stuck in our own head. Having an encouraging circle of people can sometimes make all the difference. Others in your circle may have been exactly where you are and can share some insight about what helped them. But if you don't connect with others and share what you're experiencing, they can't help.
- **Get silent and give yourself some space.** Our intuition is often trying to speak to us, but we're so distracted by all of the busyness we're surrounded with that it's hard to hear. Some answers do not come from your mind. Instead, they rise out of the stillness in a soft whisper. The only way to hear this inner wisdom is to get quiet.
- **Focus on just one step you can take today.** Don't worry about where you'll be a week, month, or year from now. Maybe you can

31

try writing from a coffee shop rather than your normal space, or learn one new exercise you can try out in the gym, or set up a meeting with your manager to discuss what you can do to improve and work toward the next promotion. Remember, just one step here—don't get overwhelmed by fast-forwarding to all of the potential subsequent steps.

No matter what, when you feel stuck, know that you'll figure it out. As Edison said, you haven't exhausted all possibilities.

Today's Prompt: Is there an area of your life where you don't know what's next? Or have you experienced a time when you didn't know what's next and come through it? If so, share what worked for you to get you to the other side.

Week 17

Just Take It Bird by Bird

"Perfection is shallow, unreal, and fatally uninteresting."

— Anne Lamott (*NY Times* bestselling author)

Have you ever thought about what you know to be true? Things change throughout our life, but what truths do we actually know, if any? As *The New York Times* bestselling author Anne Lamott neared the age of 61, she decided to write down everything she knew for sure.

In her TED Talk, *12 Truths I Learned from Life and Writing*, she shares a foundational story for her truths:

"My seven-year-old grandson sleeps just down the hall from me, and he wakes up a lot of mornings and he says, 'You know, this could be the best day ever.' And other times, in the middle of the night, he calls out in a tremulous voice, 'Nana, will you ever get sick and die?'"

Her grandson reminds us that our emotions are often mixed between a beautiful anticipation of hope and horrible anticipation of dread.

While Anne shares many beautiful truths in her talk, we'll focus on truth number six, the truth about writing. Anne states, "Every writer you know writes really terrible first drafts, but they keep their butt in the chair … the two most important things about writing are: bird by bird and really god-awful first drafts." To illustrate her point, she tells a story from her childhood about her brother, who had waited to begin a book report about birds the night before the assignment was due. Her father's advice to her brother? "Just take it bird by bird, buddy. Just read about pelicans and then write about pelicans in your own voice. And then find out about chickadees and tell us about them in your own voice."

Anne's advice applies to so many things: careers, presentations, public speaking, cooking, exercising, etc. The main point? Don't miss out on things just because you feel you're not "perfect" enough. Don't hold your true self back from the world because you feel you're not where you should be or want to be. Write and tell your stories, don't worry about your "terrible first drafts." Exercise, don't worry what you look like. Create presentations and know that you'll get better with each one you deliver. Every step you take gets you closer to where you want to be. Just take it bird by bird, buddy.

Today's Prompt: Have you held yourself back from something because you don't feel perfect enough?

Week 18

The Last Lecture

"The key question to keep asking is,
'Are you spending your time on the right things?'
Because time is all you have."

— Randy Pausch

An academic tradition for professors at Carnegie Mellon University is to give a lecture answering the question, "Hypothetically, if you knew you were going to die and you had one last lecture to give, what wisdom would you impart to others?" On September 18, 2007, Randy Pausch, a professor of computer science, gave such a lecture to his students titled "Really Achieving Your Childhood Dreams." However, in this circumstance, the question wasn't hypothetical—it was real. One month prior to giving this lecture, Randy had learned that he had terminal pancreatic cancer.

Randy's lecture is an inspirational, uplifting message with advice about how to achieve your dreams. Randy's lecture is over an hour long, so I've summarized some of his advice below:

- **Experience is what you get when you don't get what you wanted.** One of Randy's dreams was to play in the NFL. He discusses how his coach motivated him to become a better version of himself by being extremely hard on him during practice. Through this experience, he learned how much someone cares when they spend time investing in you (or giving feedback).
- **The brick walls are there for a reason.** The brick walls are not there to keep us out. The brick walls are there to give us a chance to show how badly we want something. When Randy was younger, he was inspired to become an engineer by the rides at Disney. Throughout his career, he applied to Walt Disney Imaginary many times … and received many rejection letters. It took him 15 years, but he eventually developed skills that were valuable to the Walt Disney Imaginary team and was able to fulfill his dream by working on Aladdin's Magic Carpet Ride.

35

- **Decide if you're a Tigger or an Eeyore.** Randy says, "Tiggers never underestimate the importance of having fun." Although Randy knew he was dying soon, he chose to have fun, and he believes everyone can make the same choice.
- **Have humility.** Randy's dad fought in WWII. When his mother was going through his father's things after his death, she found a Bronze Star for valor. In their 50 years of marriage, the fact that his father received this award had just "never come up."
- **Don't complain.** One day, Randy was complaining to his mother about how difficult his PhD tests were. She replied, "Just remember, when your father was your age, he was fighting Germans in WWII."
- **Value *people* over *things*.** Randy spent time with his niece and nephew every week. One week, he showed up in an expensive new convertible he had just bought. While his sister was explaining to his niece and nephew that they must be careful in the new car because it's very expensive, Randy began pouring a can of soda into the back seat. He told his sister, "It's just a thing." Later, his nephew vomited in the car due to being ill from the flu. Randy stated that he didn't care how valuable the car was, as it didn't compare to the feeling he got from making an eight-year-old boy not feel guilty because he had the flu.

Today's Prompt: Which of these pieces of advice speaks to you? Why?

Week 19

Ask the Right Questions

"I have no special talents. I am only passionately curious."

— Albert Einstein

 A company that was receiving negative customer-service reviews requested a customer-service training program that would teach their employees about the basic principles of customer service. They hoped that this would reduce the amount of negative reviews they had been receiving. The person who would be creating the training asked to speak with their employees to ask a few questions, and the company agreed.

After speaking with the employees, they found that the company had instituted a new policy about a month ago. The policy significantly reduced the amount of time an employee could be on the phone with a customer. If the employees went over on their call time, it affected their bonus. Ultimately, this led to the employees rushing through calls to make sure they could meet the new policy, which resulted in negative customer-service reviews.

The research found that the company needed to take a closer look at the call time policy instead of creating a new training program. What if the person who was to create this program didn't ask any questions? Think of all of the time and money that would have been wasted, as it wouldn't have solved the problem.

When you begin any project, the questions you ask are crucial to the success of that project. I have a particular set of questions that I've crafted over the years to pinpoint exactly what is needed and why. Sometimes, it means my services aren't needed; instead it's a whole different problem altogether. But no matter what capacity we work in, our duty is to ask the right questions to determine the best direction.

Today's Prompt: What kind of questions do you begin with when you're faced with a new project? Share questions that you've found to be invaluable.

Week 20

Perspective Is a Choice

"Things aren't good or bad. They just are."

— Author Unknown

In Eckhart Tolle's book *A New Earth*, he discusses the idea that all things are connected and there are no isolated events. He implies that the mental label of "good" and "bad" are an illusion created by our mind. This is illustrated in the story of a wise man that won an expensive car in a lottery (Tolle, 2006, p. 53):

> *His family and friends were very happy for him and came to celebrate. "Isn't it great!" they said. "You are so lucky." The man smiled and said, "Maybe." For a few weeks he enjoyed driving the car. Then, one day a drunken driver crashed into his new car at an intersection and he ended up in the hospital with multiple injuries. His family and friends came to see him and said, "That was really unfortunate." Again the man smiled and said, "Maybe." While he was still in the hospital, one night there was a landslide and his house fell into the sea. Again his friends came the next day and said, "Weren't you lucky to have been here in the hospital." Again he said, "Maybe."*

I won't suggest that I am able to not label certain things like hunger, acts of violence, etc., as bad. However, I believe the less you can label things good or bad, the more freedom you have.

A few weeks ago, I was letting a friend park his car in my garage while he was out of state and it accidentally got towed. I wish I had a video recording of myself when I went to get it and it wasn't there—total shock! There were tons of obstacles, including the fact that I couldn't get the car since I didn't own it and he was out of state. Immediately I knew that I had a choice. I could either get stressed and label the situation as bad, or use this as some awesome practice in removing the good/bad label. In the end, everything worked out and the towing company even paid the bill. So it turns out that if

I'd labeled the situation as bad and allowed myself to get stressed about it, I would have just wasted the day for nothing.

Today's Prompt: Do you believe perspective is a choice? How have you experienced this in your own life?

Week 21

Your Strengths

"Everybody is a genius, but if you judge
a fish by its ability to climb a tree, it will
live its whole life believing that it is stupid."

— Albert Einstein

A couple of times a year, I reflect on where I'm going and what strengths I believe I have that will help me in getting there. For example, when I wanted a leadership position, I wrote down every leadership quality I believe I have and how I could grow those skills.

Alternatively, I'm very aware of where my weaknesses lie. I'm not a chef. In fact, I don't even boil water. I get by on Whole Foods hot bar and eating out. Many people have seen this as a limitation and have tried to send me easy recipes and offered to come help me cook. These are such sweet offerings! However, I have no desire to cook. I know that my skills are low in this area, and I have no interest in increasing them.

During this time of reflection, I also think of others and their strengths. Knowing their strengths and weaknesses helps me to align my efforts to make us the most productive and allows us to create a positive culture in which it's ok to not be great at everything. That's why we surround ourselves with people that are different than us!

If I judged others or myself by weaknesses, the results would not be positive. But the opposite is also true. Knowing the strengths and weaknesses of those around you and yourself is an incredible skill. Praise people for their strengths and never make them feel bad about their weaknesses.

Today's Prompt: What are your strengths? Do you know what the strengths are of those around you?

Week 22

Intention

"Five seagulls are sitting on a dock. One of them decides to fly away. How many are left? Five. Deciding to fly away and actually flying away are two very different things.

Despite popular belief to the contrary, there is absolutely no power in intention. The seagull may intend to fly away, may decide to do so, may talk with the other seagulls about how wonderful it is to fly, but until the seagull flaps his wings and takes to the air, he is still on the dock. There's no difference between that gull and all the others. Likewise, there is no difference in the person who intends to do things differently and the one who never thinks about it in the first place. Have you ever considered how often we judge ourselves by our intentions while we judge others by their actions?"

— Andy Andrews

In the book *The Noticer: Sometimes, All a Person Needs Is a Little Perspective*, author Andy Andrews uses the example above to illustrate intention. How many times have we had the best of intentions, but did not act on them? What prevents us from doing what we set out to do?

If you're anything like me, it could be that you try to take on too much instead of being focused and strategic. Here are a couple of suggestions to turn your good intentions into positive results:

- **Look at your calendar.** Whatever is on your calendar is generally what you do. Be intentional about it! If your goal is to start your morning by exercising, put it on your calendar.

- **Make a list of goals or actions.** Whether it's cleaning out your basement, finishing a book you've had lying around for weeks, or signing up for a class at a local college, write it down! This gets it out of your mind so you can free up that space. Then tackle one thing on your list each week. This keeps it manageable.

Today's Prompt: What is something that you've had good intentions about but haven't followed through on? What other ways can you think of to turn good intentions into positive results?

Share the spark.
Light new kindling.
Keep the flame aglow.

Never worry about the numbers. Help one person at a time, and always start with the person nearest you.

— Mother Teresa

Help the Person Nearest You

When you think of helping others, what comes to your mind? Is it feeding the hungry, giving to the poor, or maybe traveling around the world to help provide water? Those are very noble ways of helping, but if they're overwhelming, you can help the one person nearest you at this very moment.

What a pressure relief! Mother Teresa made such an impact and it's no wonder, with the mindset of simply helping the nearest person. Whether it's helping someone expand their skillset, becoming a better leader, cooking something delicious, or simply listening to them, you have something to offer. Who is that one person you can help today?

Action: Really pay attention to your surroundings today and look for opportunities to help others. Again, don't feel pressure to do something huge. Start small! In fact, here's one concrete way to help: Invite one person to your tribe, whether it's someone you've worked with on a project, talked to in the hallway, or sit near that may not be involved yet.

Week 23

The Starfish Story

"If you think you're too small to make a difference,
you haven't spent a night with a mosquito."

— African Proverb

Have you ever heard of the *Starfish Story*? You probably have, but either way, here's a paraphrased version.

An old man took a walk on the beach every morning. One morning after a storm passed, he was walking on the beach and saw thousands of starfish on the sand.

Off in the distance, he saw a little boy walking up the beach. As the boy walked, he would bend down to pick up an object and throw it in the ocean. When the boy came closer, the man said, "Good morning! I noticed you walking down the beach and throwing something in the water. What are you doing?"

The little boy said, "I'm throwing the starfish into the ocean. The tide washed them up on the sand and if I don't throw them back in the water, they'll die." The old man said, "There must be thousands of starfish on this beach. I'm afraid you can't make that much of a difference."

The little boy bent down, picked up another starfish, and threw it into the water. He smiled at the old man and said, "I made a difference to that one!"

When I think about this story, it brings up memories of people who have made a difference in my life. Some of the seemingly small words of encouragement have truly given me the strength to keep moving. The power we have to make a difference in someone's life is remarkable. It didn't take a lot of effort from the little boy throwing the starfish back in the ocean, but what a difference he made!

Today's Prompt: Who has made a difference in your life? What did they do to make an impact on you?

Week 24

Worry Solves Nothing

"I am an old man and I have known a great
many troubles, but most of them never happened."

— Mark Twain

Merriam-Webster's Dictionary defines
worry as 'to think about problems or
fears: to feel or show fear and concern
because you think that something bad
has happened or could happen.' How
much time do you spend on problems,
fears, or thinking something bad could
happen? If you were to average it on a
typical day, how much would your
average day be consumed with
worrying?

Studies have shown the following statistics about worrying ("12 Techniques
to Stop Worrying," 2008):

- 40 percent never happens
- 30 percent has already happened
- 12 percent is needless (like what someone else thinks)
- 10 percent is petty and unimportant (like being late)
- 8 percent actually happens

Of the 8 percent that happens, 4 percent are things that are beyond our
control, such as death. The final 4 percent is the only percentage that we
have control over.

So, for the most part, you only have control of 4 percent of what you worry
about. If that's true, it's all the more reason to save your energy for the
moment you're in. The more time you spend in the moment you're in, the
less you'll worry.

Today's Prompt: Has worry ever solved something for you? What do you
do when you begin to worry about something?

Week 25

What Is Reality?

"Reality is merely an illusion, albeit a very persistent one."

— Albert Einstein

On a blustery, cold December day, I took my miniature schnauzer outside for a quick walk. While I was trying to hurry, he had other plans of finding the perfect spot in which to relieve himself, so I took a moment to watch the cars go by on the busy downtown street in front of my apartment building. At that very moment, two cars came speeding down the road side by side. As they got further down the road from me, I heard a crash and started walking toward it to make sure the occupants were okay.

Unfortunately, this was a case of road rage. As I was making my way down the street, I saw a younger guy get out of one of the cars and an older man get out of the other car. As I got closer, I saw the younger guy punch the older man and a fight broke out between the two of them. The police came very quickly, thankfully, and I walked my dog back inside. After returning outside to check on the situation, I was surprised to see that all of the onlookers who were previously outside were now gone. I was the only person left that had witnessed the incident.

The policeman asked if I would write a statement, and I agreed to do so. He stood in front of me, Witness Statement Form in hand, and paused for a moment. He said, "Before I give this to you, I want you to know that eyewitness statements are the least reliable form of testimony. If everyone who saw this incident had stayed and I took all of their statements, everyone would have said something slightly (or very) different. So just write what you believe you saw to the best of your ability." I was a bit taken aback by his comment, but shrugged it off and wrote what I saw.

A few weeks later, I found out that there was video footage of the incident. There happened to be a camera on my apartment building that recorded the entire thing. But something interesting occurred on the video. Instead of the younger guy starting the fight (like I saw), the older man threw the first

47

punch! I was shocked. From where I was walking down the street with my dog, there were several cars and a light pole between the two cars involved in the incident and me. In addition, my dog kept pulling me as I was trying to make my way to the two cars and I was preoccupied with getting him to move forward. Any of these reasons could have made me miss the first punch, causing me to catch the younger guy hitting the older guy back.

I thought back to the policeman who had warned me of this in the very beginning. And here it was, actually happening. I've spent a great deal of time reflecting on this incident and asking the question, "What is reality?" And I'm still not sure.

One thing this experience has taught me is that reality may not be what I think it is. It may just be my perspective. And now when something happens, I don't jump to "my version of reality" as quickly. I leave some room for the thought that this is just my experience of reality in this moment.

Today's Prompt: Could there be something you might be labeling as "reality" that is just your experience in this moment?

Week 26

See the Light in Others

"See the light in others, and treat
them as if that is all you see."

— Dr. Wayne Dyer

Sometimes it's easy to see the light in
people and other times it takes patience and
practice. People that bring out the best in
others are a positive dent. They change the
world one person at a time. The great news
is that you can be that person.
Opportunities to do this are everywhere!

To see the light in someone, you must first
slow down and be intentional about really
getting to know them. If you focus solely on the work, you'll miss an
incredible opportunity. Take time to build a relationship.

As you're getting to know this person, think about where you see them a
year from now. Actively pay attention to their strengths and what they
value. Sometimes, people have something in them that they can't see. It's
your role to bring this out of them.

Make sure to tell them what you see in them. These words can be life-
changing. Sometimes people are so far in their own thoughts that it's hard
for them to gain perspective about how others see them.

Don't get discouraged. Think of this time as planting a seed. It takes a while
for a plant to grow. Give grace. Be patient. In fact, you must be ok with
never seeing the end result. You may simply be a step in this person's
journey. However, that should be all the more reason to do what you can in
each moment.

Today's Prompt: How do you intentionally make an effort to see the light
in others?

Week 27

Act Yourself into Feeling

"You're more likely to act yourself into feeling,
than feel yourself into action."

— Jerome Bruner

Simply taking one small step, and then another, and then another, is sometimes the only way to make progress. This is especially true when you feel that you can't see very far into the future or you are unsure of what an outcome might be. Sometimes we allow ourselves to get overwhelmed by the unknown and simply choose to not take any action based on that. However, as today's quote suggests, our emotions do not have to dictate our actions.

As I look back at some of the most incredible events in my life, I certainly didn't feel like I was strong or had the energy to complete them. I remember feeling uncertain of how things would go, feeling the weight of what I felt was a huge obstacle, and thinking that simply not starting would be the easiest route. However, once I took a small step to propel myself forward, momentum simply came. If you wait until you *feel* ready, that time may never come. However, if you take one step, no matter how small it might be, momentum comes and feelings change.

Today's Prompt: Is there an area in which you have been waiting to feel differently before acting on the feeling?

Week 28

Feedback Is the Breakfast of Champions

"Feedback is the breakfast of champions."

— Ken Blanchard

During an interview, someone once asked me, "What feedback have you repeatedly received in your previous roles?" After thinking for a moment, I replied, "If I received feedback and did nothing with it, I'm not sure I would have lasted in my previous roles."

When someone says, "I have some feedback," do you hear "I hate you and everything you create" or "I'm going to help you elevate this to the next level"? Often, we're so close to something we create that when we receive feedback, we act like the thing is a part of us. The problem with this is that we spend a ton of unnecessary mental energy and stunt our own growth. The way feedback is given is extremely important, but the way you receive feedback is also crucial. Did you know that people who are good at receiving feedback are actually more likely to be promoted?

This also applies to relationships. Let's say, for example, that someone is continuously late when you've set a time to meet. You decide to tell him that it makes you feel unimportant when he arrives late. How he accepts this feedback may make a difference in how honest you will be with him in the future. If he gets defensive, you may choose to not bring it up again, which could potentially result in feeling resentful toward him. If he accepts your feedback and acts on it by being more conscientious of the time, you will feel better about the relationship and continue to let him know how you're feeling as things arise. This creates a healthier relationship.

Being good at receiving feedback can lead to healthier relationships, promotions, and an elevated work experience. Regularly asking for feedback allows you to be "in the know" and be the best version of yourself.

Today's Prompt: How good are you at receiving feedback? If you're good at it, what are some of your tips?

Week 29

Difficult Situations Breed Incredible Results

"Mickey Mouse popped out of my
mind onto a drawing pad 20 years ago on a train ride
from Manhattan to Hollywood at a time when
business fortunes of my brother Roy and myself were at
the lowest ebb and disaster seemed right around the corner."

— Walt Disney

 I remember sitting in my therapist's office after several months of going to her and asking, "How long am I going to be like this?!" I had been working on a lifetime of issues with her, and because I had chosen to not let myself acknowledge how I had felt for years, I had a ton of work behind me and ahead of me. I was exhausted, sad, angry, and tired of fighting. I had never experienced depression or thoughts of simply giving up until this point. Some days I couldn't get out of bed because I didn't know what the point would be or it just hurt to move.

The only thing that kept me from giving up was the belief that this period of time was temporary, like all things. So I surrendered and gave myself grace. Instead of trying to figure out the answers to all of my questions like, "Where should I live? What are we doing here? Where should I work? Will I ever date? What do I *want* to do?" I focused on taking each moment at a time. Don't get me wrong; these questions are good to ask. But if you are overwhelmed and ask them all at once, it can overwhelm you even more.

Difficult situations sometimes breed the most incredible results. Once I let go of trying to control everything and simply became grateful for each moment, things began to happen. Generally, the times that I'm most unsure of what my next step might be is when I am forced to let go and watch things unfold. The simple act of not trying to control a situation allows for creativity and possibility. It creates space for new thoughts, ideas, and people to come into your life.

Today's Prompt: Has a difficult situation ever resulted in something incredible in your life?

Week 30

The Safe Path Is Not Safe

"The safe path is not safe."

— Elizabeth Gilbert

Most of us strive for some level of 'safe.' I know I have. I've often thought about why. I remember growing up and looking around at 'normal.' Normal was graduating high school, going to college, getting a stable job, getting married, buying a house, and having children—lots of children. Then, living happily ever after ...

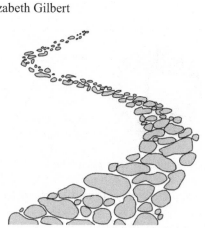

I did many of these things, but felt something was missing. The pressure to be 'normal' was a little overwhelming. It didn't come from others, but mostly myself. I would think, "Why can't you just be like everyone else? You're so ungrateful!"

For years, I wanted to start my own consulting business. In fact, I registered the name, created a website, and started a blog 4 years before officially quitting my corporate job and embarking on my own. What held me back? Self-doubt and tons of thoughts like, "How will you pay the bills? What if you don't succeed? Who will want to work with you? Do you really think you're any good? The insurance! I've heard that the insurance for individuals is a million dollars per month—I can't pay that! What if you suck and end up homeless?"

Then I thought, "What if you let all that go and just jump? Won't you always wonder?" The answer was yes. I *would* always wonder. And you know what? It worked out.

Today's Prompt: Have you ever veered outside of the 'safe path' and had it work out?

Week 31

Fear of Rejection

"If you don't ask, the answer is always no."

— Nora Roberts

 A few days ago, I went to dinner with my boyfriend. Looking over the menu, I found a sandwich that looked delicious. But then I noticed it was in the lunch section of the menu and lunch was only served until 2 PM. I complained to my boyfriend that I really wanted this sandwich, but unfortunately, it was only served during lunch. "Oh well," I said. He acted confused and said, "We'll just ask them if you can get the sandwich." I smiled and thought, "That's nice of him, but I don't need to ask—it already says 'no' on the menu!" When the waiter came back, my boyfriend asked if I could get the sandwich, and a few minutes later I was enjoying a delicious chicken parmesan sandwich. Amazing!

Why didn't I want to ask the waiter? One word: rejection. I accepted a 'no' before even asking the question. Have you ever done this? Jia Jang, creator of the video series *100 Days of Rejection*, also experienced fear of rejection, stemming from childhood. He felt that this fear was holding him back from achieving his goals. To move past his fear of rejection, he created a list and decided to actively try to be rejected for 100 days (also known as Flood Therapy).

Jia explains what happened and what he learned during these 100 days in his TED Talk, titled *What I learned from 100 days of rejection*. On the first day, he asked a man if he could borrow $100. The man said no and he scurried away. From this experience, he realized that he always ran from rejection. He decided that no matter what happened on Day 2, he would not run away.

On Day 2, he went to a local burger joint and, after eating his burger and fries, asked for a burger refill. "What's a burger refill?" the employee asked. "It's like a drink refill, but with a burger." Jia explained. After being told they don't do burger refills, he didn't run away. Instead, he told them how much he loved the establishment and that he would like it even more if they offered burger refills.

Lesson: Even though he didn't receive the burger refill, he didn't run away, which increased his self-confidence.

On Day 3, he went to Krispy Kreme, where he asked for donuts shaped like the Olympic logo. To his surprise, the staff took him very seriously and not only created this for him, but gave it to him for free!

Lesson: If you don't ask, the answer is always no.

On another day, Jia knocked on the door of someone's home, showed him a flower, and asked him if he could plant it in his back yard. The man said no. This time, Jia asked why. The man explained that his dog digs up everything and he didn't want to waste the flower. Then the man told him to go across the street to his neighbor's house. "Connie loves flowers. She'll be thrilled to see you!" the man said. Jia walked across the street to Connie's house and she did, indeed, let him plant the flower in her back yard.

Lesson: Ask why! Often we think people say no because they think we're weird or not good enough or a myriad of other reasons, but in many cases, that isn't the truth.

Today's Prompt: What is something you want, but haven't asked for? In a work situation, maybe it's telecommuting once a week, a pay raise, or taking a class to enhance your skills. In your personal life, it might be asking your significant other to go on a date night or asking for help in an area where you always just "take care of it." What is stopping you?

Week 32

Whom Have You Not Seen?

"I wonder how many people I've looked at,
all my life, and never seen."

— John Steinbeck

There are so many things you can learn about a person in 1 hour. Asking the right questions can help you get the most out of these conversations. Below are some questions that may be helpful in these meet ups:

- **We all have something that we're better at than 1,000 others. What are you incredible at?**
  This question helps you determine strengths of others and also gives them a chance to reflect on something we don't think about all of the time.
- **What is something you're learning right now?**
  This question helps you determine what excites others. Also, you or someone you may know could help them in this area.
- **What books have you recently read?**
  This question shows you what they're passionate about. Also, they may be able to recommend a book that would benefit you in some way. I've had book clubs come out of these types of questions, which gives several people a chance to dive deeper into a book and gain knowledge and wisdom from each other.
- **What would your perfect day look like? What would you be doing?**
  This is something not everyone will know how to answer. But, to get where we want to go in life, we need to know what that looks like! It's an interesting question and it may spark something in them.
- **What is an important lesson you've learned in life?**
  I love to hear people's mantras, great advice they've received, or lessons they've learned during times of struggle. There's a wealth of wisdom in these lessons.

These questions are just a start. Anything that helps you get beyond the small talk and conversation about weather is key.

Today's Prompt: What questions do you generally ask when you take time to get to know others?

KINDLING

You're braver than you believe, stronger than you seem, and smarter than you think.

— Christopher Robin

Flip this page over to take a step to connect with the world around you.

If Only You Could See
What I Can See

Some of the strongest people I've met believe themselves to be weak. For the longest time, I told myself I wasn't creative. It was a self-fulfilling prophecy; because not until I changed my perspective did I actually start creating things to help others. What if I had spent my entire life telling myself I wasn't creative? It would have been comfortable because I wouldn't have to live up to who I was created to be, but I would have cheated myself out of using the gifts that I was blessed with.

What about you? Are you telling yourself a lie to get out of living the life you were truly created to live? What if you could see yourself from someone else's perspective? Are you speaking life into others and helping them see their true self?

Action: Think of a strength you see in someone. Tell them the strength.

Week 33

She Never Ate a Shrimp

"I don't know what is best for you."

— All of Us

When my mamaw (southern term for "grandmother") passed away a few years ago, I began sobbing. Among my tears, I remember shouting, "She's never even eaten a shrimp!" One of the reasons I was sad was that I felt that she didn't truly get a chance to experience all that life had to offer. She had never traveled anywhere outside of the region where she lived, she had never flown on a plane, and she had only worked at one job  that I knew of. All of these feelings came out as "She's never even eaten a shrimp!"

My mamaw was a very predictable lady. She always had a toothpick in her mouth and would twirl it around using her tongue. I could never watch when she did this—I always imagined her choking on it! You would never catch her without a glass of sweet tea with a soaked napkin around the glass from the condensation. She made flapjacks (pancakes) in the morning and creamed potatoes (mashed potatoes) almost every day. Something about calling them "creamed" potatoes made them taste even better. She wasn't exactly the sweet, doting type of grandmother, although she loved me very much. One Christmas, I decided to be crafty (which I'm not) and make her a vase with marbles and fake flowers. When I gave it to her, she said, "What in the hell do you want me to do with this, honey?" Ah, sweet mamaw.

Over the years, I've thought about the limitations I felt her life had. And I've come to a different conclusion than I first experienced when she passed away. I'm a different person than my mamaw was. And the things I value are different. She valued consistency, familiarity, and keeping with traditions as the matriarch of our family. These things made her happy. She was a mother, grandmother, and great grandmother. And she would laugh so hard as she watched her grandchildren that she would almost fall to the floor.

I don't plan on having children, and I really want to travel, learn about different cultures, and meet lots of new people. Thankfully, my mamaw never tried to make me be someone I'm not by giving me advice that would have made her happy, but not me. And so now I no longer feel like she was living less of a life because she never ate a shrimp.

Today's Prompt: Have you ever judged someone or tried to give them advice based on what you value instead of considering what is important to them? Has anyone ever done this to you? If so, how did it feel? How might that experience affect your interactions with others who you might feel aren't "living life to the fullest," even though they are different than you?

Week 34

Become 'Unstuck'

"Everything becomes a little different
as soon as it is spoken out loud."

— Hermann Hesse

Have you ever been stuck thinking for hours about a problem and finding yourself no closer to solving it than you were when you started? What if you've already taken breaks and you're still stuck?

Sometimes asking for help is the last thing we think about. The funny thing about this is, sometimes simply stating the challenge out loud can "unstick" it from your mind so you can see it more clearly. It also requires that you organize your thoughts, because when they're in your mind, they're a bit cluttered and flying all around.

Even if stating the problem out loud doesn't help you immediately solve the problem, sometimes gaining another perspective is exactly what you need to move forward. The other person doesn't need to be super familiar with your challenge. Simply describe it and listen to their thoughts. Even if they don't have a solution, their questions may lead you to the solution.

Today's Prompt: How do you generally tackle a challenge when you're stuck? Have you ever answered your own question by stating it out loud to someone?

Week 35

The Battle You Know Nothing About

"Be kind. For everyone you meet is
fighting a battle you know nothing about."

— Wendy Mass

Over the 2017 Thanksgiving holiday, my neighbor committed suicide. He
had moved in a month prior, and although he was only in the building for a
month, everyone knew who "John" was (I've changed his name for privacy
reasons). He was a large man who wore steel-toed boots and blue jeans and
was a land surveyor, which is exactly what he looked like. He had an
incredibly gentle spirit about him, and I never saw him without a smile on
his face.

But that's not how everyone knew him. The day he moved in, he posted a
wooden sign on his door. The sign said, "In olden times, an open door
meant an invitation to come inside. If you find my door open, please come
in. You are invited."

And his door was open almost every evening. I know, because it was on my
way to the elevators to and from my apartment, and every evening I walked
my miniature schnauzer, Jacques. I would often hear laughter and chatter of
John and his company coming from inside his apartment as I walked by.
Just knowing that someone like that lived on my floor brought me great joy.

One evening, my boyfriend was on his way to my apartment. He texted me,
"I'll be there in 30 minutes." Two hours later, he showed up. He told me
that as he exited the elevator and headed toward my apartment, he passed by
John's open door and looked in. John invited him in, offered him some
scotch, and they sat and chatted like old friends. My boyfriend learned that
John had had a difficult earlier life with stints of homelessness, depression,
and most recently, a divorce. The divorce is what brought him to my
building. But he also learned that John was quite a character. He had tons of
old artifacts that he loved to share stories about and was extremely
passionate about politics.

The last time I saw John sticks in my mind like an ending to a beautiful
movie. It was Thanksgiving week. I was sitting in the lobby of my building,
writing by the fireplace. He opened the front door of the building and the

cool November air wafted in. He walked over to the fireplace to warm up and turned to look at me. Smiling, he said, "Sorry if I'm disturbing you. This fire is just so nice." And then, before I could reply, he said, "But I guess you may not mind, since I always see you sitting here as people pass by." I replied, "Exactly! If I didn't want people around, I wouldn't write in public. I love the sporadic interactions." He smiled and headed toward the elevators.

Later that week, I saw flowers on his door. They reminded me of something he would display for Thanksgiving as a tradition—I could tell he loved traditions. I've included a photo of his door with these flowers, as that is where they stayed for the days that followed. After I heard the news, I walked by them countless times and thought about what a true light of joy he was. Who else moves into a building and is known by so many within a month? Who else keeps their door open when the doors are heavy and specifically designed to stay shut? A true light in the world.

Today's Prompt: Might there be someone you might consider being a bit kinder to, since everyone you meet is fighting a battle you know nothing about? Do you have a story of a time when someone was especially kind to you during a rough time?

Week 36

Measure the Obstacle Against the Dream

"When the water starts boiling,
it is foolish to turn off the heat."

— Author Unknown

You've probably been through, going through, or will go through something difficult. Sometimes you can see the light at the end of the tunnel, and other times it feels so bleak. One of my favorite reminders of perspective is to measure the obstacle against the dream.

While writing this book, I've gone through a divorce, questioned my faith and myself, and felt the passion slip from what I thought would be my career for the rest of my life. Most of what I thought I knew is in question even as I type these words. But even in the midst of it, I absolutely know it's foolish to turn off the heat. As difficult as this period of time has been, I've learned more in it than I have in a lifetime. In fact, these experiences are what led to starting this movement.

Today's Prompt: What is something difficult you're facing? Or what is something difficult you've gone through and what good came of it?

Week 37

Coddiwomple

"Faith is taking the first step even
when you don't see the whole staircase."

— Martin Luther King, Jr.

"Coddiwomple" means to travel in a
purposeful manner toward a vague
destination. When I first stumbled across this
word, I just stared at it for a while. It came to
me at a time when I was feeling very confused
and frustrated. This word provided relief and
was such a good reminder to be in the
moment we're in, solve the problem in front
of us, and enjoy the journey.

One of my friends has a website that was
originally created to discuss the benefits of
being single. She wanted to encourage singles to practice self-care and self-
nurture, something she is always practicing. Eventually, she decided that
she wanted to teach dance (she's an incredible dancer), so she added a page
offering dance lessons. Guess who visits her website most now? Couples!
How ironic that the website she started for singles became highly visited by
couples who wanted to take dance lessons from her.

Sometimes the direction that we believe we're going is not where we end
up. For me, it often works out even better than I could have imagined. So
coddiwomple makes me think of doing everything you can do in the
moment you're in while knowing you're ultimately not in control of
everything and how things end up. It means believing that you're on the
right path and things will end up exactly as they should.

Today's Prompt: What does coddiwomple mean to you? Have you ever
experienced coddiwomple?

Week 38

Feelings Are Just Visitors

"Feelings are just visitors, let them come and go."

— Mooji

Have you ever felt sad or upset, but couldn't understand why? One day while journaling, I drew this picture (right) to describe how I was feeling. I felt very drained and heavy. My mind was in overdrive, and I felt paralyzed in making any decisions. I also felt confused as to why I was feeling this way. It seemed like my mind had wrapped itself into a messy ball and the ball weighed a ton.

So I asked myself two questions:
1. What are you feeling? Name the emotion.
2. Why might you be feeling this way?

By allowing myself to sit still, become calm, and just "be," I was able to get in touch with the root of the issue. I found that when I stopped thinking so much, took a deep breath, and answered the question "What are you feeling?" I realized that I felt sad. I instantly felt a little lighter just by recognizing the emotion that I was feeling. After asking myself why, I simply wrote what came out and then realized where the sadness was coming from. I could breathe again! I felt lighter! Instantly. While it took me a few hours of feeling exhausted and heavy to decide to try this exercise, this practice of just recognizing and acknowledging how I was feeling changed everything. Now whenever I feel this way, I instantly sit down, get out my journal, and write out the answer to those two questions.

Today's Prompt: What do you do when you're feeling upset, sad, angry, etc.? Might you consider asking yourself today's questions next time you experience these feelings?

Share the spark.
Light new kindling.
Keep the flame aglow.

It has been said something as small as the flutter of a butterfly's wing can ultimately cause a typhoon halfway around the world.

— Chaos Theory

The Butterfly Effect

In a speech about the Butterfly Effect, Andy Andrews, *The New York Times* bestselling author, states, "Consider that even the simplest actions matter beyond measure—they matter forever. A kind word, a smile, a challenge, listening, simply being in someone's presence ..." He goes on to share how over 2 billion lives were saved due to a simple act of kindness.

Action: Watch the 10-minute YouTube video titled "The Butterfly Effect," by Andy Andrews. Then, take a moment to remember you are connected to everyone and everything. Every choice you make matters.

Week 39

Rise Above the Critics

"It is not the critic who counts; not the man who points out
how the strong man stumbles, or where the doer of deeds could
have done them better. The credit belongs to the man who is
actually in the arena, whose face is marred by dust and sweat
and blood; who strives valiantly; who errs, who comes short
again and again, because there is no effort without error and
shortcoming; but who does actually strive to do the deeds; who
knows great enthusiasms, the great devotions; who spends
himself in a worthy cause; who at the best knows in the end the
triumph of high achievement, and who at the worst, if he fails,
at least fails while daring greatly, so that his place shall never
be with those cold and timid souls who neither know victory
nor defeat."

— Theodore Roosevelt

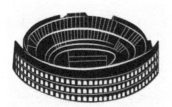

Theodore Roosevelt gave "The Man in the
Arena" speech on April 23, 1910. He
believed that one learned by doing, and
that it is better to stumble than sit and
criticize those who are actually doing
something.

Today's Prompt: Might you ever have unfairly judged someone who
stumbled, yet were at least trying to do something? What thoughts do you
have about today's quote?

Week 40

Today Is My Favorite Day

"What day is it?" asked Pooh.
"It's today," squeaked Piglet.
"My favorite day," said Pooh.

Some days I forget to think about the small things that I am grateful for. They come in many forms and experiences, like:

- Sitting by the fire and reading a book
- Having a deep, meaningful conversation with a friend
- Receiving an unexpected compliment
- Successfully finishing a project
- Looking up at the vast night sky when it is full of brilliant colors and hues of pinks and blues and feeling full of hope at the greatness of it all
- Hearing a favorite song
- Smiling at strangers on the street and hearing them say, "Good morning!"
- Holding a warm beverage like tea or coffee and watching the steam flow through the air
- Watching my dog run around excitedly when I say "treat treat"
- Connecting with someone who I haven't seen in a long time
- Sitting in a dimly lit restaurant, sipping wine, and eating a delicious meal

Something good happens every day. What are some of the small things that you are grateful for?

Today's Prompt: What are some ways that today could be your favorite day?

Week 41

Circle of Safety

"Every single one of us should look at our managers/leaders of the companies we work for and ask ourselves, 'Would I want to be in a foxhole with you?' And the managers/leaders of companies who rely on us, should, in turn, ask themselves, 'How strong is our company if the answer is no?'"

— Simon Sinek (*Leaders Eat Last*)

In his book *Leaders Eat Last*, Sinek discusses the idea of a Circle of Safety. Basically, the idea is that there are tangible, extremely effective benefits when teams focus on helping each other and building trust instead of competing to get to the next level.

There are many external dangers to a business, including fierce competition, but if the people inside a company don't feel safe, they can't use their energy to mitigate the external dangers. They'll spend most of their energy trying to protect themselves from each other. But once a Circle of Safety is established, they can invest their time and energy to guard against the dangers outside.

In the book, he demonstrates how this looks in many corporations as well as the military, and he discusses tangible benefits. The main habit in cultivating a Circle of Safety is empathy. When people know that you see them and they feel like they're heard and understood, it helps cultivate the Circle of Safety.

A tangible benefit of this Circle of Safety is the fact that people are more likely to speak up and share their ideas without feeling judged or being afraid that someone would steal their idea. This leads to more effective teams and, ultimately, a more successful organization.

Today's Prompt: How empathetic are you? Do you have a Circle of Safety? If not, what is one thing you could do to begin cultivating this?

Week 42

You Are Wonderful

"If you see something beautiful in someone, speak it."

— Ruthie Lindsey

Glenn Van Ekeren, author of *12 Simple Secrets of Happiness*, shares a true story about the power of kind words and encouragement. A Paris opera house was sold out in anticipation of a famous singer who would be performing.  Unfortunately, on the day of the performance, the singer fell ill. At the beginning of the event, the announcer had to be the bearer of bad news and let the audience know that the singer was ill, and instead, they would be hearing a stand-in. The crowd went from excited chatter and anticipation to groans of disappointment and frustration.

The stand-in singer did an incredible job, but he simply wasn't whom the crowd came to see. When he finished his last song, instead of sounds of clapping, an uncomfortable silence followed. Not a single person applauded. Suddenly, a little boy jumped up and shouted, "Daddy, I think you are wonderful!" After hearing this, the crowd erupted into roaring applause.

Imagine the feeling this father experienced because his son spoke up. One small act of love, six simple words, changed the entire environment.

Do you know that you are wonderful today? You are. There isn't another you. Move forward in the day knowing that. And if you see something beautiful in someone today, speak it.

Today's Prompt: Have you seen something beautiful in someone recently? What was it? Did you tell them?

Week 43

Are You Moving Too Fast?

"For fast-acting relief, try slowing down."

— Lily Tomlin

One warm evening, Sir Isaac Newton had dinner with a friend. After dinner, they decided to sit outside under the shade of apple trees in his garden. During this time there wasn't a multitude of distractions like cell phones, TVs, iPads, computers, etc. So Newton and his friend were simply "being" in the garden. Every now and then, an apple would fall to the ground. Since Newton was paying attention to his surroundings, he noticed this and thought to himself, "Why does the apple always fall down, instead of sideways or up? Why is it pulled to Earth's core?" The revelation of gravity ultimately came from this thought.

While there are a few renditions of this story, the point of today's thought is that simply spending time "being" can bring about incredible revelations. A few days ago I tried watching a movie and, before I knew what I was doing, I was checking Facebook on my phone! In this world full of constant distractions, we're so used to rushing around that the concept of slowing down is a little foreign (and a little difficult). When I ask people how they're doing, most of them say, "I'm just so busy!" I've not come across anyone who has said, "I'm just really bored." While I'm not saying that always being bored would be a good thing, I am saying that for most of us, we must be intentional to take time for ourselves and simply "be."

When was the last time you allowed yourself time to exist distraction-free and reflect on whatever came to mind? This might be:
- Sitting on your front porch, sipping tea, and gazing at the sunset
- Spending a weekend in a mountain cabin with no TV or phone
- Laying by the ocean, listening to the waves, and breathing in the ocean air

- Sitting in a coffee shop, sipping coffee/tea while journaling, and watching passersby

Sometimes we spend so much time running from one thing to another, stressing out about a situation, we forget that slowing down and reflecting can actually bring about the revelation we so desperately need. We put so much emphasis on doing that we forget about being! In fact, research has found that these types of passive activities, which some might describe as boredom, actually increase creativity. Being bored gives you the insight into what may need to change and the time and space to tackle a problem or try something new.

Whether you need a breakthrough in your personal or work life, being "bored" may be just the solution you need.

Today's Prompt: Are you moving too fast? Or are you great at allowing yourself periods of time with no distractions to reflect and be creative?

Week 44

The Impediment to Action Advances Action

"The impediment to action advances action.
What stands in the way becomes the way."

— Marcus Aurelius

In the book *The Obstacle Is the Way*,
Ryan Holiday shares how to overcome
obstacles and turn them into
opportunities. Holiday illustrates this by
sharing dozens of stories from
legendary icons such as Steve Jobs,
Abraham Lincoln, and Thomas Edison.

So often we put all of our effort and
energy into getting rid of an obstacle
instead of realizing that it's an
opportunity to grow and using it to our
advantage. This is an incredible perspective shift!

For example, if you're unhappy with your job or a relationship situation,
how could you turn this obstacle into an opportunity? Maybe the culture on
your team is something you're unhappy about and you're supposed to play
a role in making it better. Maybe your relationship with your partner is
feeling stagnant and some growth needs to occur. Maybe you're feeling
distant with a friend and need to have a conversation that would ultimately
lead to you becoming closer friends than you ever were. Whatever stands in
the way *becomes* the way.

Today's Prompt: What is one obstacle you're currently facing in your
personal or work life? How can you use it to your advantage?

KINDLING

I always wonder why
birds stay in the same place
when they can fly anywhere
on the earth. Then I ask
myself the same question.

— Harun Yahya

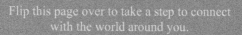

Flip this page over to take a step to connect
with the world around you.

Travel!

One of my friends speaks fondly of his travels around the world. At one time, he lived in Cambodia while on a mission trip without knowing the language. Each day he would ask his Cambodian companion who spoke very little English, what they would be doing that day, and his companion would always say, "You'll see." Determined to learn the language, he worked hard to understand and speak it and eventually became fluent in it. He has tons of crazy, fun stories from his time there.

Traveling to different places and learning various cultures gets us out of our comfort zones. It grows us in a way that we can't grow in our familiar surroundings. Learning a new language while immersed in a different culture is certainly one way to grow!

When was the last time you took a trip somewhere? This world is full of new experiences just waiting to be discovered! Your experience doesn't have to be visiting a new country. It can be as simple as going on a road trip a couple of hours away.

Action: Plan a trip, large or small, to see and learn something new! If you're already great at traveling, take someone (who doesn't travel as often) with you.

Week 45

We're Closer Than We Were

"We're closer than we were."

— Pat King (my mother)

When I was little, I would ask the typical question that a lot of kids ask on a road trip. "Are we there yet?" My mother would always reply with the same five words, "We're closer than we were."

Sometimes, when I'm struggling through something, I think about these words. When I look back and see how far I've come in a particular area, I remember that I'm closer than I was.

All of us have "closer than we were" areas. What is an area of life in which you may not be where you want to be, but can recognize your progress? It could be a project you're working on, a relationship, perspective, fitness, etc. Acknowledging how far you've come is a crucial part of the journey.

Today's Prompt: Share an area where you are "closer than you were."

Week 46

What to Do When You Are Unhappy with Your Situation

"Change the changeable, accept the unchangeable,
and remove yourself from the unacceptable."

— Denis Waitley

In Eckhart Tolle's book *The Power of Now*, he explains how to be in the moment:

"Wherever you are, be there totally. If you find your here and now intolerable and it makes you unhappy, you have three options: remove yourself from the situation, change it, or accept it totally. If you want to take responsibility for your life, you must choose one of those three options, and you must choose now. Then accept the consequences."

When I reflect on my own life experiences and those of loved ones, the times when we complain without taking any action are the most frustrating—for us, and everyone involved. Have you ever known someone who constantly complains about his or her job, but won't do anything about it? Have *you* ever been that person? Let's say that we don't like our job because we have too much on our plate and we're feeling stressed. If we apply today's advice to this situation, we have three options:

1. **Change the situation.** This could mean compiling the laundry list of projects/tasks we have and asking our manager to help prioritize the list.

2. **Accept the unchangeable.** Maybe this is a particularly busy time of the year, and we know there is a light at the end of the tunnel. So we accept it temporarily, as it is currently unchangeable.

3. **Remove yourself from the unacceptable.** If it's been this way for quite a while and you've tried to change the situation but there is no relief in sight, it might be time to remove yourself from the unacceptable.

These three options can be applied to every situation, whether it's a relationship you're unhappy in, a commute that is taking too much of your time, a living situation that isn't quite working for you, etc. When you feel yourself getting frustrated about something, remembering that these are your options can help you move forward with the best approach for the situation. The worst thing you can do is complain about something that is bothering you, yet take no action.

Today's Prompt: Is there something that is currently upsetting you where applying these three options may be helpful?

Week 47

Yesterday's Junk

"You can't reach for anything new if your
hands are still full of yesterday's junk."

— Louise Smith

Yesterday's junk can sometimes be comforting, especially if you've held onto it for a long time. It can be scary to get rid of it. It can also be painful, because it means you have to face it and deal with it. Your junk could be how someone treated you in the past, how you see yourself, a relationship with someone, or anything that holds you back from being your true self.

I've had my share of junk that I've held onto because of the fear of the unknown. I wasn't sure what life without it would feel like. It felt almost like a security blanket to keep it. I've had other people point out some of my junk and urge me to deal with it. But I wasn't ready at the time.

When I decided to purge a bunch of my junk, it wasn't a deliberate choice. I simply felt unhappy and decided to explore why. After making the first decision to take a closer step to happiness, things snowballed. Getting used to the security blanket being gone was a painful and scary experience. I've sat in therapy and dealt with issues I'd rather not deal with. I can remember in one session asking, "Is this the rest of my life? Will I keep coming in here and talking about this crap? Will it never end? I'm exhausted and I'm tired of dealing with this."

Now that I've moved through some of this junk, I feel lighter. I have more space around me. I am more open to new ideas and, because I'm not weighed down by the junk of the past, I can explore and embrace those new ideas.

Today's Prompt: Do you have any junk from yesterday that is holding you back from reaching something new? If so, what step might you take to remove this junk?

Week 48

Horrible, Awful, No-Good Days

"Why are you laughing, mom?" — Patti Bryant (age 5-ish)
[laughing hysterically] "So I don't cry, honey!" — Pat King
(Patti's mom)

Some days are a struggle. Sometimes there's no reason for it. It might go something like this: You wake up, put lotion in your hair, step in water while wearing socks, your dog poops on the carpet, you lock your keys in the car, you have trouble communicating with people all day, your technology stops working, and you just feel beat up at the end of the day.

As I've gotten older and have these types of days, I reflect on how my mom would just start laughing for what seemed like no reason when I was much younger. In fact, I find myself doing the same!

So what can you do when the day is a struggle? Here are some options:
- **Laugh.** Sometimes we take things too seriously. Laughing can take the stress out of a situation. If I get in such a poor mood that I can't make myself laugh, I'll often look up funny videos.
- **Surround yourself with space.** Taking the entire day off isn't always an option, but I've noticed that when I'm having a day where I fumble around and can't seem to do anything right, I need some space. Sometimes it means sitting quietly or meditating for a few minutes. Sometimes it means taking a nap. Sometimes it means getting out in nature or going on a walk.
- **Turn on some music.** Have you ever noticed that your mood changes when you listen to a song you love?
- **Exercise.** As much as I dislike exercising, it helps!
- **Journal.** It might seem unhelpful to focus on how miserable you feel and write about it, but often it can feel like a big sigh of relief. Keeping things bottled up can make your fuse even shorter.

Sometimes naming the emotion by simply writing something like, "I am so angry!" can take all the power out of it.

- **Read/Watch/Listen to something encouraging.** I suggest reading/watching/listening to something that doesn't really expect you to perform an action, but instead is simply for your enjoyment. You've already got a ton of things to do and adding another thing when you're having a bad day isn't helpful.

And ultimately, a day only lasts 24 hours, anyway.

Today's Prompt: What do you do on horrible, awful, no-good days?

Week 49

Doubt vs. Failure

"Doubt kills more dreams than failure ever will."

— Karim Seddiki

 The definition of doubt is 'to be uncertain about; consider questionable or unlikely; hesitate to believe.' Negative self-talk is like the spark that fuels the flame for doubt. The more you tell yourself things like, "There's no way you'll be able to do that. Who are you kidding? You better prepare yourself for the worst because you're going to be disappointed if you don't," the more you fuel doubt.

Is your self-talk positive or negative most of the time? If it's negative, have you ever wondered why you can't just believe the best in situations instead of automatically doubting yourself? Your brain has neural pathways that are like a dirt road that's been traveled so often that it's left a clear path. If you've dealt with negative self-talk a long time, it's because *that's* the path that's easiest for the brain to travel.

But you can change the road! If you want to make progress in beginning to remove doubt, there are some exercises that you can do to begin to carve a new path to positive self-talk. One thing that's helped me is spending time being still and observing when a thought that makes me doubt myself occurs, and then being intentional about stating something positive about myself. After doing this repeatedly, I've found that it's much easier to believe the best because I've changed the path.

There are many resources that will help you carve new, positive neural pathways that remove doubt about yourself and eliminate negative self-talk. If this is an area where you need help, find something that works for you.

Today's Prompt: Do you tend to doubt yourself or believe in yourself? If you tend to doubt yourself, what actions might you take to change your neural pathway and shift into believing in yourself more?

Week 50

What Are You Missing?

"The little things? The little moments? They aren't little."

— Jon Kabat-Zinn

On a cold January morning at a metro station in Washington DC, a man started to play the violin. Thousands of people walked by the violinist, as it was during rush hour and people were on their way to work.

While there were thousands of people who walked by him, almost no one stopped to listen. A three-year-old stopped and stared, but his mother briskly moved him along. Everyone was in such a rush to get to their destination that they simply didn't have time to take a moment for themselves.

When the violinist stopped playing, he was met with a dull silence of busy passersby. No one clapped or even noticed him. In the entire 45 minutes he played, only six people stopped to listen. He received $32 in tips.

The violinist was actually a world-famous performer, Joshua Bell. Earlier that week he had played in Boston to a sold-out crowd, where people paid $100 a ticket to see him perform. This was a social experiment conducted by *The Washington Post* to determine, among other things, if we stop to appreciate beauty or recognize talent only when it's convenient to do so.

Have you ever missed out on something because you were too busy or distracted? It could have been a whole period of your life when you were so overwhelmed that you simply didn't have the capacity to see the beautiful things all around you. Or it could be that you've missed out on a simple "Bye, I love you" from a significant other because you were in your own thoughts at the time.

I often get in what I call "work mode," where I'm not enjoying the journey, but instead am focusing directly on the outcome or destination. When I'm in work mode, my shoulders tighten, my whole body feels tense, and I don't notice anything going on around me. Small problems often feel much larger and overwhelming. It's a stressful state of mind and can sometimes be difficult to recognize when I'm in it. Thankfully, my boyfriend can instantly recognize it. If I'm just finishing with work and seem distracted as we head to dinner, he'll say, "I see you're in work mode." For some reason, calling this by name instantly removes some of its power. I'm able to get out of work mode even quicker once it's identified. This brings me back to a state of enjoying the little things: a starry night sky, a beautiful flower, my happy dog, a simple conversation, a smile from someone, the way the sun feels on my skin, a hot shower, etc.

It takes effort and focus to notice the little things. It may require creating some space in your schedule. It may also require you to say "no" to a few things so you can move a little more freely throughout your day. But as today's quote suggests, the little things aren't little. In fact, there's nothing bigger.

Today's Prompt: How good are you at noticing the little things? If you're stressed and finding it difficult to notice them, what could you potentially do differently to free yourself up?

Week 51

Focus

"People think focus means saying yes to the thing you've got to focus on. But that's not what it means at all. It means saying no to the hundred other good ideas that there are. You have to pick carefully. I'm actually as proud of the things we haven't done as the things we have done."

— Steve Jobs

 In the book *Made to Stick*, Dan Heath and Chip Heath introduce a military concept called Commander's Intent (CI). The CI is basically an end goal for a given situation. Though they create thorough plans, the military understands that many plans do not survive contact with the enemy. So the CI makes the end goal very clear to everyone involved. If someone needs to improvise to achieve the goal, they do.

CI can be used in business, as well. In fact, you can probably identify the CI in many successful businesses. Steve Jobs focused on very few products and making them beautiful, while his competitors spent their energy on tons of products. Below is an example from *Made to Stick* of how Southwest Airlines uses CI (Heath, C., & Heath, D., 2007):

> *Herb Kelleher [the longest serving CEO of Southwest] once told someone, "I can teach you the secret to running this airline in thirty seconds. This is it: We are THE low-cost airline. Once you understand that fact, you can make any decision about this company's future as well as I can.*

> *"Here's an example," he said. "Tracy from marketing comes into your office. She says her surveys indicate that the passengers might enjoy a light entree on the Houston to Las Vegas flight. All we offer is peanuts, and she thinks a nice chicken Caesar salad would be popular. What do you say?"*

The person stammered for a moment, so Kelleher responded: "You say, 'Tracy, will adding that chicken Caesar salad make us THE low-fare airline from Houston to Las Vegas? Because if it doesn't help us become the unchallenged low-fare airline, we're not serving any damn chicken salad.'"

CI can also be used in your personal life to help you make decisions. What is the CI in your life right now? It could be healthy living, encouraging others, getting a degree, etc. You may have a couple and it can change based on your season of life. Whatever it is, once you know it, every decision you make can be based on it. This will help you to determine which things to say no to and keep you focused each day.

Today's Prompt: What is one Commander's Intent for your personal or work life right now?

Week 52

I Appreciate You

"A person who feels appreciated will
always do more than what is expected."

— Author Unknown

In my emails, I often use three little words
to convey a message to folks: "I appreciate
you!" This seems like such a simple,
ordinary phrase, but the reaction I've seen
from it is astounding. One person recently
replied, "This is the nicest thing anyone has
told me all week!" Another person wrote,
"Thank you—I needed this!" It turns out
that people actually don't hear this a lot.
This is unfortunate, since I'm sure they are
appreciated, but we are often so busy that
it's sometimes hard to remember to act on
the appreciation we feel for others.

As today's quote suggests, I've also had
people reply to this phrase and offer even more help than they originally
offered, such as "Oh, and here's a link to the entire images folder, in case
that is helpful." While getting folks to do more isn't the reason to make
them feel appreciated (people can easily identify fake praise), it certainly
doesn't hurt!

Whether you're a leader and want to motivate employees, someone who
wants to motivate his or her significant other, or a parent who wants to
motivate his or her child, there are several ways to show appreciation.

- **Be specific.** People like to be noticed, and often they don't feel
  noticed. Saying something like, "I noticed how quick you were to
  respond to that client. Thank you for taking care of that for us!" or
  "Thank you for taking the kids out to play so I could have a quiet,
  peaceful moment. I appreciate you!" or "Look at this bedroom! I
  appreciate the incredible job you did cleaning your room!" can
  really make someone's day. It also reinforces their behavior and

lets them know that it's something you appreciate so they'll continue to do it.

- **Surprise them.** Giving someone a little surprise lets them know you were thinking of them. Not sure what to give? Food is often a great place to start! In a work environment, this might be bringing in some homemade brownies, giving a Starbucks gift card, or taking them out to lunch. Whatever is appropriate, little surprises are always a nice touch.

- **Return the favor.** Everyone has good days and bad days. Take time to notice when these are and go out of your way to help others when they need it. For example, the colleague that was so quick to respond to a client on the team's behalf may need help with something another day. Or the significant other who took care of the kids so you could have a moment of peace may need a nap break one day. Returning the favor is a tangible way to show your appreciation.

Today's Prompt: What are some ways that you currently show appreciation for others?

Reference List

Heath, C., & Heath, D. (2007, January 2). *Made to Stick: Why Some Ideas Survive and Others Die*. New York, NY: Random House.

Holbrook, C. (2008, September 24). *12 Techniques to Stop Worrying* [Blog post]. Retrieved August 01, 2016, from http://www.pickthebrain.com/blog/stop-worrying/

Mayo Clinic. (n.d.). *Stress management*. [Blog post]. Retrieved August 01, 2016, from http://www.mayoclinic.org/healthy-living/stress-management/in-depth/stress-relief/art-20044456

Tolle, E. (2006, September 1). *A New Earth: Awakening to Your Life's Purpose*. New York, NY: Penguin Group.

Made in the USA
Monee, IL
21 July 2020